Political & Economic Systems

DEMOCRACY

David Downing

Heinemann Library
Chicago, Illinois

Customer Service   888–454–2279

Visit our website at www.heinemannlibrary.com

Designed by AMR
Originated by Dot Gradations
Printed in Hong Kong by South China Printing

07 06 05 04 03
10 9 8 7 6 5 4 3 2

Library of Congress Cataloging-in-Publication Data

Downing, David, 1946 Aug. 9-
  Democracy / David Downing.
      p. cm. -- (Political and economic systems)
Includes bibliographical references and index.
  ISBN 1-40340-317-1
  1. Democracy--Juvenile literature. [1. Democracy.] I. Title. II.
Series.
  JC423 .D693 2003
  321.8--dc21
                        2002006318

Acknowledgements
The publishers would like to thank the following for permission to reproduce photographs:
Bridgeman/Musee Carnavalet, p. 4; Popperfoto/Apichart Weerawong/Reuters, p. 5; Bridgeman/British
Museum, p. 6; Corbis/Ruggero Vanni, p. 8; Bridgeman/Lincoln Cathedral, p. 10; Bridgeman, pp. 12,
20; Corbis/Francis G. Mayer, p. 14; Corbis/Geoffrey Taunton, p. 17; Hulton Archive, p. 22;
Popperfoto/Juda Ngwenya/ Reuters, p. 23; PA Photos/EPA, pp. 24, 36, 50; Rex/Nils Jorgensen, p. 26;
PA Photos, p. 29; Popperfoto/Simon Kwong/Reuters, p. 30; Corbis/Steve Raymer, p. 31;
Corbis/Bettmann, p. 32; Popperfoto/Danilo Bartulin/Reuters, p. 34; Popperfoto/Paul
McErlane/Reuters, p. 37; Rex/SIPA Press, p. 38; Stone/Adrian Murrell, p. 41; Corbis/Wally McNamee,
p. 43; Popperfoto/Eriko Sugita/Reuters, p. 45; Corbis/Sergio Dorantes, p. 47; PA Photos/EPA Pool
Reuters/Jerry Lampen, p. 48; Corbis/Peter Turnley, p. 53.

Cover photograph: Supporters of Nelson Mandela in the first post-apartheid elections in South Africa,
1994, reproduced with permission of Corbis.

Every effort has been made to contact copyright holders of any material reproduced in this book.
Any omissions will be rectified in subsequent printings if notice is given to the publishers.

Our thanks to Christopher Gibb for his comments in the preparation of this book.

Some words are shown in bold, **like this.** You can find out what they
mean by looking in the glossary.

Contents

① Turning Points

At the beginning of 1789, France was ruled by King Louis XVI. There was a little-used French **parliament** called the States-General that included representatives of the three so-called estates, or classes (the clergy, the nobility, and the common people), but it had no real power.

Everything changed that summer. On June 17 the Third Estate, representing the common people, declared itself a new National Assembly. Three days later, locked out of their usual meeting hall, the representatives met in an indoor tennis court, where they signed an oath to stay together until France had a **constitution** based on the will of the people.

This is the meeting in the Parisian tennis court, as painted by the famous French artist Jacques-Louis David.

The king tried to reassert his authority, but on July 14 a mob stormed the Bastille, a prison in Paris, and he was forced to withdraw his troops from the city. In the weeks that followed, the new National Assembly abolished the social and economic system, divided the country into *départments* ruled by elected assemblies, and drew up a Declaration of Rights. This said that **sovereignty,** or power, lay with the people, not the monarch. France had crossed the line that separates a **dictatorship** from a democracy.

The events of that summer were an important turning point in the long history of democracy. There have been many others. The French Third Estate had been influenced by the American Revolution a decade earlier, and throughout the next century, people struggling for democratic rights would find inspiration in both of these revolutions. The twentieth century opened with the struggle to win the vote for women in many countries, and as the century drew to a close, the nations of eastern Europe celebrated the fall of **communism.** Millions watched on television as Nelson Mandela walked away from prison, victorious in the long struggle to create democracy in South Africa. In May of 2002, Myanmar's Aung San Suu Kyi, a supporter of democracy in a military-ruled society and the recipient of the Nobel Peace Prize, was released from house arrest, where she had been held for nineteen months.

FOR DETAILS ON KEY PEOPLE, SEE PAGES 59–60.

It has not always been easy for democracy, of course. The murder of pro-democracy protesters in Beijing's Tiananmen Square in June of 1989 was also shown on television around the world. There has been no shortage of men and women prepared to suffer imprisonment and worse, rather than succumb to dictatorial governments. As the 21st century began, many brave campaigners for democracy remained under arrest.

Aung San Suu Kyi, the leader of the Myanmar pro-democracy movement, greeted supporters outside her house in July of 1995.

② An Idea in Waiting

Imagine a group of prehistoric men gathered around an evening fire, discussing the question of where they would hunt on the following day. These are the tribe's older, more experienced hunters, and they all feel qualified to put forward their point of view and have it listened to. Here by their fire, these men are taking part in a democratic process, not because they like the idea of democracy, but because it seems like common sense to make use of everyone's experience.

Greek democracy

Small independent groups like this, and the sense of natural equality that flourished within them, eventually fell victim to the larger communities that came with the spread of agriculture and permanent settlements. In these communities, power was not shared so equally, and there was no place for democracy. For several thousand years, most societies were ruled by **monarchies, dictators,** or small groups of individuals (oligarchies).

Democracy, the process of involving citizens in government, resurfaced in several city-states in what is now Greece around the end of the sixth century B.C.E. It was probably the citizens of Athens who coined the word *demokratia* (democracy)—a combination of *demos* (the people) and *kratos* (to rule)—to describe their system of government.

This marble statue is of the Athenian leader Pericles, an early champion of democracy.

The central feature of this system was the Assembly, a regular mass meeting where those who were considered citizens could have their say. The Assembly elected ten generals to run the military, but the ruling council of 500 members (the Boule) and other public officers were chosen by a lottery in which all citizens had an equal chance. Since those chosen could only serve for a limited period, every citizen had a good chance of being selected at least once in his lifetime.

Other citizens' rights were necessary for the system to work in the way it was supposed to. The most important of these rights was free speech. Without it, there could be no real debate in either the Assembly or the Boule.

Early limits to democracy

There were definite limits to the sort of democracy that was practiced in Athens and other Greek city-states, limits that would also apply to many democratic systems right down to the present day. The franchise, or right to vote, was given to all citizens, but not to all adults. Women, slaves, and foreigners were not considered citizens, and therefore only a quarter of the adult population actually took part in the democratic process. Also, the rich continued to have ways of influencing events which were not available to the poor—like bribing elected officials—regardless of how equal they were supposed to be as citizens.

The importance of free debate

"Our ordinary citizens, though occupied with the pursuits of industry, are still fair judges of public matters ... And instead of looking on discussion as a stumbling-block in the way of action, we think it an indispensable preliminary to any wise action at all."

(Athenian politician Pericles, explaining in 431 B.C.E. how important free discussion was in reaching the right decisions.)

7

FOR DETAILS ON KEY PEOPLE, SEE PAGES 59–60.

Even this limited democracy worried famous **philosophers** such as Socrates, Plato, and Aristotle. They all feared that the poor were too stupid or irrational to be given such responsibility. They preferred the idea of rule by the wise and the politically skilled, by men who knew what the people wanted better than the people themselves. The thinkers of the time believed that well-meaning but undemocratic governments should act as parents or guardians, acting in their people's best interests whether the people wanted them to or not. This idea has lingered on through the centuries.

The Roman Republic

Greek democracy only lasted a few hundred years, finally dying out around the second century B.C.E. During this same period, the Roman Republic also flourished, and while not a democracy in the Greek sense, it had democratic characteristics. After an early period where only the aristocrats—men who had inherited positions of power—took part in government, the common people were allowed to hold some offices and elect their own leader.

These are the ruins of the Roman Forum, where democratic assemblies were held in the years of the Roman Republic.

When the Romans began to conquer other lands, the newly conquered people were allowed to become Roman citizens and, in theory, share in these democratic practices. In reality, the expansion of Roman rule over such a vast expanse of territory made it impossible for most of these citizens to have any real influence on the government, which remained in Rome. The idea of sending representatives from the regions to the capital never caught on.

By the last century B.C.E., the Republic's democratic institutions had been destroyed by **corrupt** officials and power-hungry soldiers. The Republic itself was replaced by a dictatorial Empire. For the next 600 years, democracy more or less disappeared.

New assemblies

Democracy reappeared in northern Europe around C.E. 600. In order to settle disputes and discuss new laws for their communities, groups of Vikings would call an assembly or *Thing*. They were not inspired by memories of Greek or Roman democracy. In fact, they had probably never even heard of it. They were simply acting as people who regarded each other as equals.

Around C.E. 930, the Vikings on Iceland created the *Althing,* an assembly for the whole island, which lasted for more than three centuries. Over the next 500 years similar regional and national assemblies came into being throughout Scandinavia. Similar bodies also made their first appearances in England and other European countries, but in these places the principle of equality only played a small role in their creation. The expansion of manufacturing and trade had brought about a new and wealthy business class, and the traditional rulers of these countries—usually **monarchs**— were often in need of money.

As the centuries went by, these rulers, instead of risking violent opposition by simply taking what they wanted, would usually put together an assembly of the rich and powerful. These people would then decide how to arrange things in a way that would benefit themselves as well as the ruler. In their early years, these assemblies represented only one small section of society, but as time went on an increasing proportion of the population would, for a variety of reasons, be allowed to take part.

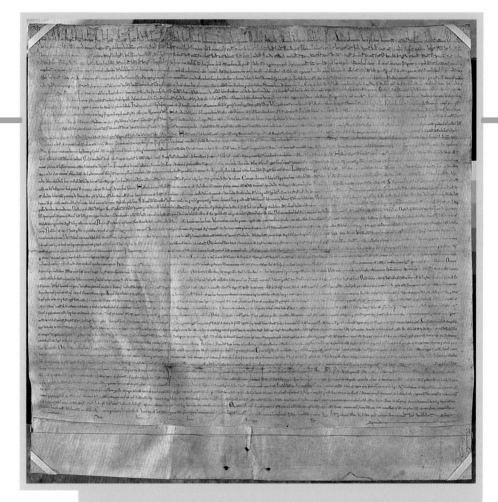

This is a copy of the English Magna Carta (Great Charter), the document limiting the powers of the monarchy, which King John was forced to sign at Runnymede in 1215.

The British Parliament

A good example of one of these assemblies was the British Parliament. This had two chambers, or Houses.

The original group of rich and powerful **nobles** that the king consulted became known as the **House of Lords.** The representatives of the property-owning middle class were elected by the people, and became known as the House of Commons, which soon developed into the more powerful of the two chambers. Working both separately and together, these Houses slowly managed to limit the authority of the king until the system reached what seemed like a natural balance of power and a natural division of tasks. The system worked like this: Parliament proposed new measures and laws (the **legislative** function of government) and the king made sure that they were carried out (the **executive** function). When it became necessary, independent judges interpreted the laws (the **judicial** function). Each of these three powers was a check on the other two.

This system was not set up as a response to a popular demand for democracy. It was just the way in which the various groups at the top of the society shared their power. However, the people who wished to expand government representation to those beyond the upper classes—and who wanted to further limit the powers of the king (who represented no one but himself)—were happy to call themselves supporters of a greater democracy. The idea itself was further strengthened by the rise of **Protestantism.** If, as some Protestants believed, all humans were equal in God's eyes, then surely they should also be equal when it came to choosing and running governments.

11

In Britain, these threads came together in the seventeenth century. Charles I, a stubborn king, tried to reduce the power of Parliament. This sent the country into a **civil war** that cost him his throne and his life: he was beheaded in 1649. During the civil war, the idea of a democracy that involved all the people was given a huge boost. One particular group, the Levelers, made some shocking suggestions. They argued that all men should have an equal vote in annual elections, that those elected should carry out the people's instructions rather than think for themselves, and that members of Parliament should serve only two terms in a row. Proposals like these, as impractical as they may have been, were in tune with the spirit of the long-vanished Greek democracy.

The Putney debates

In October and November of 1647, the winners of the English Civil War held a series of political debates at Putney, outside London. One of the Levelers, Colonel Rainsborough, argued for universal male suffrage (the right to vote for all men). "I think it's clear, that every man that is to live under a government," he said, "ought first by his own consent to put himself under that government." The more conservative General Ireton disagreed. He thought the vote should be restricted to those men who owned property.

King Charles I is shown here entering the House of Commons to arrest five members of Parliament in January of 1642. They had already escaped. Civil war between the king and Parliament broke out three months later.

The Levelers were defeated, and the monarchy was restored in 1660. The new deal which was struck between Parliament and the monarchy—the so-called Glorious Revolution of 1688—kept the common people out of the political process. By this time, many other countries had assemblies or parliaments, but, as in England, fewer than five percent of the population was allowed to vote. All of these assemblies either lacked real political power or were entirely composed of the rich and privileged.

Most of the rich and privileged, like the Greek philosophers of old, imagined that democracy was just another word for mob rule and did everything they could to oppose it. Most ordinary people accepted this state of affairs, and there wasn't much demand for increased participation in the political process. As the eighteenth century unfolded, there was no real sign of the democratic revolutions to come.

Political thinkers

In the seventeenth and eighteenth centuries, several influential studies of government were written in Britain and France. The most important of these were John Locke's *Two Treatises of Government* (1690), the Baron de Montesquieu's *The Spirit of the Laws* (1748), and Jean-Jacques Rousseau's *The Social Contract* (1762). Although very different, each recommended greater democracy, and each later influenced many of those involved in the American and French revolutions.

③ Representative Democracy

In the last quarter of the eighteenth century, the American Revolution (1775–83) and the French Revolution (1789–94) placed the idea of democracy at the center of the world stage.

Each revolution was a response to what was seen as **tyranny.** Supporters of each claimed that the people should be able to choose a different government than the one they had.

The American colonists, who felt that they were paying taxes to a distant country that did not allow them any say in its decisions, coined the phrase "no taxation without representation." The Declaration of Independence they signed in 1776 emphasized that governments only held their powers by the consent (agreement) of the people who were being governed. In France, the Declaration of Rights proclaimed that the source of all **sovereignty** lies in the nation. At the time, these were deeply democratic revolutions.

Leaders of the American colonies sign the Declaration of Independence.

After overthrowing the previous systems of rule, the revolutionaries tried to come up with new, democratic systems to replace them. This was not an easy or straightforward task. The United States and France now had many important decisions to make. These decisions would determine how user-friendly, long-lasting, and democratic their democracies would be.

How representative?

Since there was no chance of getting the entire adult male population of either France or the new United States into one city square, the direct democracy that had worked well in the Greek city-states—where issues were discussed and decisions made by all involved—was clearly out of the question. The new systems would have to be **representative democracies,** where the mass of the population would elect only a few of their people to represent their views in the new assemblies.

This shift from direct democracy to representative democracy was considered unavoidable by everyone, but some political thinkers still worried that democracy would be damaged in the process. After all, democracy was supposed to be about bridging the gap between governments and the governed. Wouldn't a new gap open up between the people and their representatives?

Thinkers such as Tom Paine and James Mill suggested that frequent elections might help prevent the representatives from growing away from the people. Paine and Mill argued that if representatives had to keep winning elections, then they were more likely to listen to what the electors (the common people) had to say. Like the Levelers, they believed that representatives should only serve a limited number of terms.

What did representing a group of people actually mean? Was the representative simply supposed to follow the instructions of the majority who voted for him? Or was he expected to use his own judgement? If he was supposed to use his own judgement, then how far could his judgement differ from that of the people he was supposed to represent? The possibility that free representatives—without frequent elections, limited terms, or obedience to their electors' wishes—would eventually form themselves into a permanent political class with its own interests, separate from those of the people, worried thinkers like Paine and Mill.

Others, like Alexander Hamilton, disagreed. They liked the fact that representative democracy placed a gap between government and people, and that it allowed the well-educated and well-informed representatives to make the decisions, instead of the poorly educated and poorly informed common people. This gap prevented democracy from turning into the mob rule they were

The inevitable answer

"Since all cannot, in a community exceeding a single small town, participate personally in any but some very minor portions of the public business, it follows that the ideal type of a perfect government must be representative."

(English political thinker John Stuart Mill, the son of James Mill, writing in 1861.)

afraid of. It allowed the creation of a political class that could rule wisely on the people's behalf.

A political class

The tension between these two groups has continued to this day. One is always pushing for greater democracy, while the other tries to keep democracy within what it considers sensible limits. In general, those who wished to limit democracy have had their way. Elections are usually held at intervals. For example, the presidential election in the United States is held every four years.

This statue of John Stuart Mill is in London's Temple Gardens. Like his father, James Mill, John Stuart Mill was an influential political thinker.

This can seem like a long time to those who want more influence over the decision making. The number of terms a representative can serve are rarely limited, with the notable exception of the U.S. president, who since 1951 has only been allowed two terms in office.

In most countries, representatives have indeed formed themselves into a political class that is usually divided into two or more political parties. This political class—or political elite, as it is sometimes called—is sometimes criticized for only paying close attention to the people during election times. Each party devises and offers a package of programs and policies that it thinks the electorate (those who vote) will find appealing. The one that wins the most votes gets the chance to put into effect as many of those programs and policies as it wants. This is the representative democracy that is used in countries like the United States and Britain. It is different than the model favored by people like Tom Paine and James Mill.

④ Constitutions and the Franchise

There is a lot more to setting up a **representative democracy** than simply electing a **legislative assembly** to debate new policies and laws. How will the executive branch (the branch of government that puts these new measures and policies into practice) be chosen? How will the three-way relationship between **legislative, executive,** and **judiciary** work? How much power will this central government have over administrations functioning at the city and state levels? Each nation's answers to these questions are laid out in its **constitution.**

The British system

The British political system evolved gradually over hundreds of years, and bore the marks of the **monarchy's** long losing struggle with **Parliament.** In the seventeenth century, the elected body took over the legislative powers, leaving the monarch to function as the executive arm of government. In the eighteenth century, the monarch was forced to hand over most of this remaining power to a prime (first) minister. By the nineteenth century, the monarch's role was almost entirely symbolic.

Sovereignty now rested in Parliament, which elected its own executive arm of government. This was headed by a prime minister, who appointed ministers to head the various government departments. Since Britain is a relatively small country, there wasn't much pressure for strong regional rule and a unitary system rather than a **federal** one was adopted. In a unitary system, the central government always has the final say.

The fact that the British system was not built to certain standards, but simply changed over time, has left it with some old-fashioned characteristics.

There is no written constitution, no bill of rights, and, in theory, the monarchy retains some power. Since judges and some other members of Parliament are not elected, the executive branch must be trusted not to abuse the powers it holds.

The U.S. system

The U.S. citizens who set out to frame a constitution for the United States in the years after the revolution were eager to adopt and improve upon the better parts of the British system. They were also determined to get rid of the old-fashioned parts. In particular, they did not want to create their own monarchy. They decided instead on a republic, with a separately elected executive presidency.

Declaration of democracy

"We hold these truths to be self-evident, that all men are created equal, that they are endowed by their Creator with certain inalienable Rights [rights that cannot be taken away], that among these are Life, Liberty, and the pursuit of Happiness. That to secure these rights, Governments are instituted [set up] among Men, deriving their just powers from the consent of the governed."

(The beginning of the Declaration of Independence(1776). It was written by Thomas Jefferson, who later served as secretary of state, vice president, and president.)

One of these constitution-makers, the future president Thomas Jefferson, wanted to create a system in which the various arms of government—the legislative Congress, the executive presidency, and the judiciary (headed by the Supreme Court)—would act as checks and balances on each other's power. This separation of powers would prevent any of the three branches of government from abusing its power.

FOR DETAILS ON KEY PEOPLE, SEE PAGES 59–60.

This system was built to specific standards. It was written down, and it included a bill of rights. Due to the nation's huge size, there were significant differences in interests, outlook, and culture in the various regions. Because of these differences, a federal system in which each of the states in the Union retained significant powers, was considered appropriate. In the event of a dispute between the two levels of government (for example, when certain southern states refused to accept federal laws banning racial segregation) the Supreme Court would be asked to decide in favor of one side or the other.

Thomas Jefferson wrote the Declaration of Independence and later served as president of the United States (1801–1809).

These two systems—U.S. presidential democracy and British parliamentary democracy—have both stood the test of time. Each works in its own way, and each has been imitated over the last 200 years. Other countries have introduced variations on the two themes, sometimes combining what they see as the best features of both, sometimes leaving out those elements that they think are no longer relevant. All the Scandinavian countries, for example, have done away with the second or upper chambers which both Britain (the **House of Lords**) and the United States (the Senate) retain. Other countries have added a bill on social and economic rights to existing bills of political rights.

Expanding the right to vote

The other great issue that faced the revolutionaries of the late eighteenth century, and one that continues to provoke heated debate and violent struggles to this day, was the extent of the franchise, or the number of those who had the right to vote. These days we assume that all adults should be able to vote, but this was far from clear to those who took part in the American and French revolutions.

The **French Revolution** initially offered the vote only to people with a certain amount of property, and a decision in 1793 to introduce universal male suffrage (votes for all adult men) was never brought into use. Many people in the United States wanted universal male suffrage as well, but those who wrote the new constitution also insisted on a property restriction. More U.S. citizens owned property than in Europe, but close to 40 percent of adult white males were still denied the vote. Women and slaves were excluded altogether. Women were granted the right to vote in 1920, and it was not until the 1960s that many descendants of slaves were actually able to use their right to vote.

A protester, supporting the women's right to vote in Britain, clings to the railings of Buckingham Palace in an effort to resist arrest.

Throughout the nineteenth century, the franchise in the most developed countries was widened at regular intervals. In Britain, for example, the percentage of adult males entitled to vote rose from 5 percent in 1831 to 100 percent in 1918. However, each of these advances was met with opposition. The upper and middle classes' fear of mob rule was slow to fade, and philosophers such as John Stuart Mill argued that rule by the common people posed a terrible threat to individual liberty. He suggested that elections should be less frequent, and that better-educated people should have more votes.

In the developed world of North America and northwestern Europe these arguments were finally lost early in the twentieth century. In these parts of the world, most countries had adopted universal male suffrage (votes for all men) by the beginning of World War I and universal female suffrage by the beginning of World War II.

By the middle of the twentieth century, in the developed countries of the West, rich and poor alike had come to consider democracy the only truly acceptable form of government. Other countries were encouraged to follow their example. Toward the end of the twentieth century, the collapse of both European **communism** and South African **apartheid** were seen as important steps along the road to a democratic world.

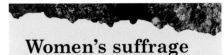

Women's suffrage

Women received the right to vote in these countries in the following years:

New Zealand	1893
Australia	1902
Finland	1906
Russia	1917
Canada	1918
Germany	1919
United States	1920
Great Britain	1928
France	1944

Black South Africans line up to vote for the first time in April of 1994, after the collapse of apartheid.

⑤ Voting

Voting has always been an important feature of any democratic system. In ancient Greece it was done by a show of hands, a method that is still used in many meetings. In modern politics, however, where even a minor local election involves thousands of people, votes are cast at an officially supervised polling (voting) station. The details of the procedure vary from country to country, but typically the voters put a mark next to the name or names of those they wish to represent them, and place their completed voting or ballot papers through a slot in a sealed container. Machines are commonly used in the United States, and voters punch holes in cards to register their choices.

Most long-time democratic countries operate a **secret ballot.** The names of voters are checked by officials, but their names do not appear on the ballot papers, so no one knows who voted for whom. This secrecy was enforced (in Australia in 1856, Britain in 1872, and the United States in 1884) because an open ballot meant that people could be pressured into voting for someone, such as a landlord or employer, who had power over them.

This is what it looks like inside a voting booth in the United States.

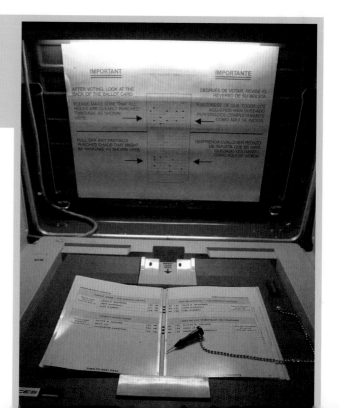

Political parties

In most cases, people vote for an individual who represents a political party. Individuals can still get elected on their own merits, but since the eighteenth century, the dominance of political parties has become increasingly overwhelming.

Political parties were started because people who agreed with each other on the issues of the day joined together for practical reasons. As well-organized groups, they were much better equipped to raise money, fight elections, and operate in the elected assemblies.

Referendums

In some democratic systems, some decisions—particularly those that involve changing the country's **constitution**—are thought to be too important to leave to **representative democracy.** Instead, in the manner of ancient Greece, the people as a whole are given a direct vote. Such votes are called referendums (or sometimes plebiscites), and are usually decided by a simple majority. For example, the British people were asked in 1973 to vote in a referendum on whether or not Great Britain should join the European Economic Community. (They voted yes.)

Like representative democracy itself, parties were necessary for democracy to work in a large modern society. In most cases, individuals could join the political party of their choice, attend local meetings and national conferences, and become involved in debating, deciding, and promoting the ideas and policies that their party supported.

What have parties stood for? Sometimes they reflect the interests of economic groups or classes. For example, in the 1930s the Democratic Party in the United States came to represent the interests of the working class. It promoted policies that it believed would support and defend those working-class interests. The Labor Party in Britain had similar policies.

Those parties were considered left of center—or more liberal—on the political spectrum. The major parties that opposed them at that time—the Republicans in the United States and the Conservatives in Great Britain—were considered right of center because, among other things, they were more pro-business, more opposed to government intervention in the economy, and more inclined to place individual freedom before the needs of the community.

The political terms "left" and "right" have traditionally offered a rough guide to what parties believe about a whole range of important issues. Democracy is not one of these issues. Both left and right parties have been democratic and undemocratic at times.

The British Labor Party meets annually to discuss issues important to them. In most democracies, major parties hold conferences like this to discuss their policies.

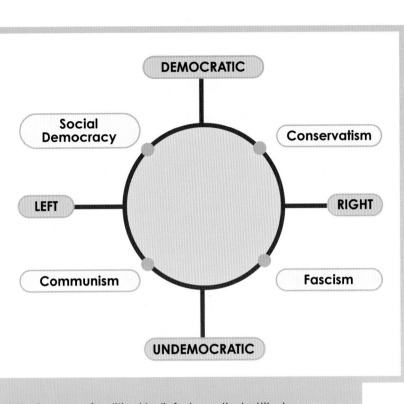

This diagram of political beliefs shows that attitudes toward democracy can differ widely among those of both the left and the right.

Electoral systems

Organizing a system of voting is also a difficult task, and many different systems have been used over the years. All of them involve voting in a particular area—a Congressional district in the United States, or a parliamentary constituency in Britain or France—but the similarities end there. In some cases, one representative is elected from the area; in others, two or more are elected. In some cases, a representative needs to win more votes than any other single candidate. In other cases, a representative must win more than 50 percent of the vote.

There are many variations of electoral systems, but only two main types. In the system that is used in British general elections (and U.S. presidential elections), the candidate who wins the most votes in an electoral district is elected. This means that if Party A received 51 percent of the votes, then it would win 100 percent of the seats in the assembly; if Party B received 49 percent of the votes, it would receive no seats at all. In such circumstances, the makeup of the elected parliament would not reflect the votes of all the people.

Fortunately for this system, regional differences in wealth, party support, and many other factors mean that opinions are never spread that evenly. However, this system can sometimes produce exaggerated majorities. In the election in Britain in 2001, the Labor Party secured a landslide (overwhelming) victory with fewer than 40 percent of the votes actually cast. The system also works against smaller parties—like the Green Party in the U.S.—which may be popular throughout the country but cannot manage a winning level of support in any particular group of people.

The other major type of electoral system, which is widely used in continental Europe, is **proportional representation,** or PR. This can be set up in a number of different ways, but the main point is to ensure that the number of votes cast fully reflects the number of assembly seats won. One way of doing this is by creating electoral districts with a higher number of representatives. For example, each party will

Electing a U.S. president

In the United States, presidents are elected by a two-step process. People in each state vote for a presidential candidate. They also vote for a number of electors to send to a national electoral college (assembly). The members of this electoral college then formally elect the president by voting for the candidate with the highest popular vote in their state. The 2000 election between George W. Bush and Al Gore showed that it is possible under this system for a candidate (Gore) to win a majority of the nationwide vote, yet fail to secure a winning majority in the electoral college.

make up a list of ten candidates, and if a particular party wins 30 percent of the vote, then the top three names on their list will be elected.

After the votes have been counted, a victorious candidate—in this case, Glenda Jackson of the Labor Party—celebrates her election to the British parliament.

Since, in this situation, a party would only need 10 percent of the votes to have a representative elected, PR tends to increase the number of political parties with a chance of power. This certainly allows more views to be expressed, but those who favor the first system argue that PR has significant flaws of its own. Voters can elect representatives who reflect their views more accurately, but these representatives then have to make deals with other parties, which hold different views, to form a government. Since these governments are formed by a group of people who disagree with each other, they tend to be weak, short-lived, or both.

Supporters of PR reply that whatever its weaknesses, their system does a better job of reflecting the actual will of the people, and is therefore more democratic.

29

⑥ The Crucial Ingredients

When **communist** parties were in power in eastern Europe (1947–89), elections were held on a regular basis. Voters were allowed to take part in a secret ballot to choose between candidates for local and national assemblies. In some countries these candidates even represented different political parties. Were these countries that called themselves "people's democracies" truly democratic?

The answer is no. These communist countries had set up a democratic system, but they did not provide the people with the other ingredients needed to make the system work in a democratic way.

Free elections and freedoms

The first of these ingredients is the existence of fair elections. Elections need to provide voters with a real choice between parties offering different programs. They must be supervised by elected officials who have no personal interest in who wins or loses, who can be trusted to make sure that no one votes more than once, and who count the votes honestly and accurately. This was rarely the case in the communist countries of eastern Europe, and cannot always be taken for granted in even the more developed countries of the West, as was demonstrated in Florida during the presidential election in 2000.

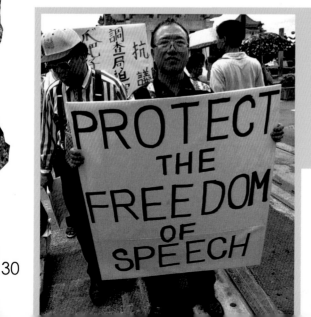

This man is demonstrating for freedom of speech in Taipei, the capital of Taiwan, in May of 1999.

A second group of even more important ingredients are the freedoms of expression, assembly, association, and the press (newspapers, radio, and television) that allow democracy to function. These freedoms provide the environment that democracy needs to flourish. So what are they? Freedom of expression allows issues to be debated, governments to be criticized, and alternatives proposed. Freedom of assembly permits people to gather for discussions like this. Freedom of association allows them to join together in parties or pressure groups to get their views across. These three freedoms make it possible for the people to join in the democratic process.

Freedom of the press—press not controlled by the government in power—should provide the information people need to make their own democratic choices. Without freedom of the press, and without the wider freedom of expression (in conversation, books, and films), it is often hard for people to know what is actually happening, and even harder for them to make informed decisions about how they should best vote to achieve the society they desire.

A range of newspapers can be bought in a Western democracy. For a democracy to work well, people must have access to a wide range of opinions.

The rule of law

Another crucial ingredient, which is often taken for granted in those countries with a long tradition of democracy, is the **rule of law.** It does no good for a government to allow all the above freedoms to

Freedom of speech

"If all mankind, minus one, were of one opinion, and only one person were of the contrary opinion, mankind would be no more justified in silencing that one person, than he, if he had the power, would be justified in silencing mankind."

(From John Stuart Mill's book *On Liberty*, published in 1859.)

flourish if it is prepared to override them at moments of crisis. In China in 1957, the communist leader Mao Zedong encouraged the people to speak out with the slogan "Let a hundred flowers bloom, let a hundred schools of thought contend [do battle with each other]." There was so much criticism of the government that the experiment was soon stopped, and many critics found themselves in jail. Most seriously of all, it made the Chinese people afraid to criticize their leaders, even when encouraged to do so. For the freedoms to flourish, people must trust that those freedoms will always exist, and they can only do that when those who have the job of upholding them (the judges and police, in particular) cannot be pressured by governments into setting them aside.

This photo shows Beijing's "Democracy Wall" in April of 1980. Local residents read a nine-page poster denouncing a new clampdown on China's pro-democracy movement.

No perfect scores

None of the ingredients listed above were significantly present in the so-called people's democracies of eastern Europe. Individual freedoms were limited, the media was heavily restricted, and the rule of law operated only at the communist party's convenience. Most of the new governments that have developed in those countries are more democratic. They have joined that process of global democratization that has been proceeding slowly for several centuries, but they cannot be expected to become fully democratic overnight. Even those countries that have been improving their democratic institutions for two centuries still fall short of that.

The rule of law

'Wherever law ends, tyranny begins.'

(The political philosopher John Locke, emphasizing, in his *Two Treatises on Government* that the rule of law is essential to democracy.)

In these democratic countries—with occasional exceptions—the rule of law operates, individual freedoms are upheld, and elections are conducted fairly. However, there has often been very little to choose from between the major parties. In the United States and Great Britain, for example, recent elections have usually been contested by two major parties committed to the defense of a free enterprise society with limited government intervention in the economy.

This lack of choice has not often been challenged by the media. The newspapers, radio, and television stations, though largely free of government control or interference, are mostly owned by the rich and powerful, who share the main parties' interest in opposing far-reaching change. Democracy works in these countries, but it is far from perfect.

33

7 Fertile Soil, Stony Ground

Democracy is not like an electric light that is either on or off. It is like a light with a dimmer switch. It can certainly be turned off, but it can also shine at varying degrees of brightness. The crucial ingredients discussed in the last chapter (free and fair elections, the freedoms of expression, assembly, and association, and the **rule of law**) must be present, at least to some degree, for the light to shine at all, but there are several other important factors that can cause it to fade or blaze brightly.

Physical threats

One important consideration is the presence or absence of a direct physical threat to the democratic system. Such a threat can come from inside or outside the country, from the overwhelming political, economic, or military might of other states, or the country's own armed forces and police.

The history of the twentieth century has many examples of large states weakening or destroying the democracies of smaller ones. Both the United States and Great Britain have been guilty of standing in the way of democracy in other countries.

Chile's democratically elected communist president, Salvador Allende (third from right), is shown here during the military coup that led to his overthrow and death in September of 1973.

The United States played a role in overthrowing the democratically elected governments of Guatemala (in 1954) and Chile (in 1973), and replacing them with pro-U.S. military **dictatorships.** Great Britain refused to recognize the independence of India—which they had run as a colony since 1858—until 1947. The British presence in India prevented Indians from democratically governing themselves.

Other countries, particularly in the **developing world,** have faced a similar threat from their own military forces. In Nigeria, for example, the attempt to create a working democratic system has been continually interrupted by military takeovers. Here and elsewhere, the motives behind such takeovers are mixed: sometimes a simple want of power, and other times a desire to stamp out the **corruption** that a young and inexperienced democracy has encouraged. Whatever the motives, democracy cannot be expected to thrive when the country's army is effectively holding a gun to its own head. In a democratic system, the military must always be under the control of the elected government.

No coincidence

The Central American country of Costa Rica has not had any armed forces since 1949. It is also the only country in Latin America that has maintained a continuous record of democratic government since World War II.

A democratic culture

The belief that the military should be subject to civilian control is deeply ingrained in older democratic countries like the United States and Great Britain. It is part of the democratic culture, the set of beliefs held by the vast majority of the population that supports democracy.

Put simply, the people of these countries believe that the only acceptable way of doing things is the democratic way. This is not a new idea for them. They have inherited a long tradition of democratic thought and practice. It would take a huge crisis, a complete breakdown of the way the current society operates, to make people question this democratic tradition and the way they live and govern themselves. The democratic culture in such countries is strong.

General Sani Abacha, leader of Nigeria's military government, inspects an honor guard in 1996. Nigeria has since returned to civilian rule.

In other countries, of course, democratic culture is weaker or even nonexistent. When varied political and economic crises erupted between World Wars I and II, Italy and Germany—whose democratic culture was not well established—gave in to the argument that a strong dictatorship would be better suited to make things right.

Today, there are still countries, such as China, that have no historical experience of democratic rule. Even if democratic institutions are introduced in such places, a democratic culture will need decades to establish itself.

It is also worth remembering that democracy means the rule of the people, not simply the rule of the majority. Governments, of course, are usually run by the party that has won the most votes; but in a truly democratic culture, they must also take the wishes of the minority into account. In Northern Ireland, for example, the **Protestant** community has always been in the majority. Most outsiders now believe that over the years it has often used this dominant position to keep the minority Catholic population from having any say in the way the province is run. Without a strong democratic culture, democracy can easily become the **tyranny** of the majority.

In October of 2000, a woman walks past a mural glorifying the Protestant paramilitary group, the Ulster Freedom Fighters, in Belfast's Shankill road.

Shared values

It is usually easier for one group of people to accept the opinions of another group if both groups share the same basic values. Similarly, in countries with a population that shares values, culture, and a single ethnic background, it is often easier for people to accept those governments that they have not actually voted for. Democracy is not seen as a possible threat because everyone in the country shares and accepts the same way of life. Until recently, this situation existed in most European countries.

If countries are divided between ethnic, religious, or linguistic (language) groups, and basic values are not shared, then there may be problems. Democracy is built around the idea of compromise, of accepting that sometimes we don't get the government or the policies we want. However, people are often unwilling to compromise when it comes to their most basic values.

Elizabeth Rehn, a United Nations special reporter for human rights in Bosnia, visits a field outside Srebrenica that is littered with the remains of Muslim refugees slaughtered by Serbs in July of 1995. The various cultures in Bosnia found it impossible to settle their differences peacefully or democratically.

If members of a large minority culture feel that their interests are being ignored or opposed by members of a majority culture, then that minority may stop supporting the country's democratic system.

There are ways of getting around these problems. Until recently, for example, the United States successfully persuaded immigrants from a variety of cultures to adopt a new set of shared American values. Countries divided along ethnic or national lines, like Belgium and Switzerland, have adopted **proportional representation (PR),** which allows each national community a **veto** (the right to reject a proposal) under certain circumstances. This makes it almost impossible for any one culture to dominate the others. In some cases, a **federal constitution** has provided minorities with additional protection; in others, having some powers of self-government has provided minorities with the right to make at least some decisions for themselves.

As a last resort, minority cultures can decide that no such compromises are possible and seek to set up countries of their own. Such attempts sometimes succeed (the creation of Slovakia, for example, following the breakup of Czechoslovakia in 1993), but often they are successfully opposed, as when the southern states of the U.S. attempted to leave the Union in 1861.

A lack of other options

Fascism offered aggression, racism, and an economy that relied on producing arms. **Communism** sacrificed democracy in return for centrally planned economic growth, and ended up with neither. Military and other dictatorships after World War II have been brutal and unsuccessful. Those who believe in democracy can argue that despite all its failings in practice, it still seems far better than any of the alternatives in the twentieth century.

A measure of equality

In a democracy, all citizens are supposed to have equal political rights: the same number of votes, the same right to run for election, and the same access to information. No one should have more influence on the decision-making process than anyone else.

Unfortunately, this political equality is often weakened by economic inequality. Even in the longest-established democratic systems, the rich can buy favors from politicians with their financial contributions, decide what will be discussed, and influence debate through their ownership of the media. In younger, less well-established democratic systems, the likelihood of bribery and **corruption** is usually much higher, because people are not used to honest behavior in politics.

When the French historian Alexis de Tocqueville wrote his famous book *Democracy in America* in the mid-nineteenth century, he made the point that, at the time, the gap between rich and poor was much narrower in the United States than it was in Europe. He thought this social and economic equality was the reason why U.S. democracy was doing so well.

The market economy

Democratic conditions have only existed for a long time in countries with **capitalist** or **market economies,** those where most of the property is privately owned and where most of the goods are bought and sold in a free marketplace. This supports the belief that such economies create favorable conditions for democracy. However, those same market economies also create conditions that can limit democracy.

Market economies have proved themselves more efficient at producing growth than anything else. Societies that can afford to spread the wealth around are usually more tolerant and more inclined to accept those compromises that make democracy possible.

Such economies produce strong middle classes that are likely to value education, personal participation in the political process, and the rule of law. All of these are vital to a healthy democracy. Most importantly, market economies put most economic decisions in the hands of individual consumers and producers rather than in the hands of the government. It is very hard to imagine political democracy flourishing in an economy where all decisions are made by the government.

Despite the positive effects, market economies can produce high levels of economic inequality that are harmful to democracy. The rich get a better education, better access to information, and more chances to influence those in power. In such a situation, the political equality that has been built into the democratic system becomes more and more meaningless.

To deal with this problem, governments have introduced measures designed to narrow the gap between rich and poor, or at least to prevent it from widening. The rich have money taken from them in higher taxes and the money is used to give the poor increased support, or welfare benefits. In some countries, rules have been established that limit the amount of money that citizens can contribute to political campaigns. This prevents what amounts to the buying of favors. A huge gap between rich and poor remains, however, and it is bad for the democratic process.

A wide range of housing can be seen in Bombay, India, where there may be a distance of only a few hundred feet between extreme poverty and wealth. This is the case in large cities around the world.

⑧ Strengths and Weaknesses

For most of the last 2,000 years, democracy has been strongly criticized. The great thinkers of their times thought that common people were too stupid to rule, and the rich and powerful were too scared of losing their wealth and positions to give them the chance. Yet over the last 100 years, all that has changed. Democracy has been adopted in most of the world's richer countries and continues to spread. These days, people frequently complain about abuses of democracy or a lack of democracy, but rarely about democracy itself.

Strengths

Democracy gives the people a voice. It allows them to both select and reject their government. The governments of today's **representative democracies** often hold enormous power between elections. They sometimes behave in a **dictatorial** manner, but in the end they are accountable to the electorate—the people. They know that if they are cruel or unable to do the job, they can be voted out.

A positive view

"Democracy is the superior form of government, because it is based on a respect for man as a reasonable being."

(From John F. Kennedy's 1940 college thesis, published as *Why England Slept*.)

Democracy could not happen without freedom of expression, and freedom of expression can only be guaranteed in a democracy. In a democratic society, people are usually free to do much more than just vote for political representatives. They are also free to learn what they want to learn, live where they want to live, and have the job they want to have.

Freedom also means responsibility, and in a democratic society people are expected to take responsibility for their own lives. Since they have at least some control over the actions of their government, people cannot say they have no power, or claim they are just following orders. Sharing in the decisions means sharing in the responsibility. In a political sense, and perhaps also in a human sense, democracy can make people grow up.

Democratic countries tend to be more peaceful, at least when it comes to dealing with other democratic countries. Democratic governments are more used to the idea of solving conflicts through compromise. Their business people have a lot to lose if disputes and conflicts interrupt trade. Most importantly, democratic politicians are forced to recognize their citizens' unwillingness to risk injury and death.

Democratic governments have continued to fight wars in the **developing world,** but even here public opinion has limited the military options. Since the United States suffered so many casualties in the Vietnam War, the U.S. government has been extremely reluctant to order any military action that might result in the death of American citizens.

Many anti-Vietnam war demonstrations took place in the 1960s and 1970s.

Democracy also usually produces wealth and prosperity. **Market economies** and political freedom support and are supported by democracy. Both grow well where an independent **judiciary** enforces the **rule of law,** where information is widely available, where there is no political interference in education, and where creativity is allowed to flourish.

Weaknesses

Democracy also has weaknesses. One already mentioned is the way in which democratic rule can become the **tyranny** of the majority in situations where basic values are not shared. It is easy to find examples of where this has occurred, and equally easy to suggest voting systems and constitutional arrangements that might give the minority community a bigger say in their government. **Proportional representation** would at least ensure that the minority was represented in an elected assembly. For example, the two communities could agree to share power by making sure that the minority's representatives were always put in charge of some government departments. Of course, if the majority community is unwilling to recognize the minority community, any of these changes would only have limited effectiveness.

A cynical view

"Democracy substitutes election by the incompetent many for appointment by the corrupt few."

(British playwright George Bernard Shaw, in his play *Man and Superman*, 1903.)

Another practical weakness lies in democracy's inability to act swiftly and decisively when such action is needed. For example, it is hard to imagine that Stalin's decision in the early 1930s to prepare the Soviet Union for a probable German invasion would have ever occurred in a democracy. Stalin sacrificed millions of people with his crash program of industrialization that was carried out in terrible conditions, although it may have saved the world from the tyranny of **Nazi** Germany.

Governments elected for a few years are very aware that they must face the electors in the not-too-distant future. They are often reluctant to make decisions necessary for the country's long-term benefit if they believe that doing so will damage their prospects of winning the next election. Those same governments sometimes borrow and spend large amounts of money on popular projects to help them win the next election, knowing that it will be future governments and generations who will have to pay the bill.

Japanese children from Kyoto hold up a model "planet of life" at the December, 1997 conference on **global warming.** Maintaining popularity with voters can be more important to democratic governments than working for results that may take longer to achieve, such as those agreed to at this conference.

45

A final weakness of national democracy, perhaps the most serious it faces, has only developed in recent years. Democracy exists within countries at every level, from local clubs to national governments, but it does not often reach out across national boundaries. This was not a problem when the important political and economic decisions were made at the national level. Unfortunately for democracy, that is no longer the case.

A realistic view?

"The tragedy of modern democracies is that they have not yet succeeded in effecting [bringing about] democracy."

(French political thinker Jacques Maritain, writing in 1940.)

⑨ Beyond the Nation-State

Since the rise of the nation-state, it has been assumed that governments have the right to exercise authority within national boundaries. When these governments were elected democratically, it meant that the people of those countries had the final say over what happened. Beyond the boundaries of the countries, however, no one held authority. Agreements were reached between countries, but they were not written laws and there was no international agency to enforce them. Democratic and non-democratic countries could only live in relative harmony for the simple reason that they rarely came into contact with each other. There was trade between nations, but there were very few truly international businesses.

All this has changed. Over the last 50 years there has been a fast-growing spread of business, culture, and communications around the world. This spread is called globalization. By the end of the twentieth century, only 49 of the 100 largest economies on earth were the economies of single nations. The other 51 were multinational corporations, businesses operating in several countries. World economic and technological development has created a situation in which the flow of money, goods, services, and even culture across national boundaries has increased greatly. These flows, when they are controlled at all, are controlled by multinational corporations—not by governments.

This 1980s photograph shows young women at work in a factory of the multinational Reebok company outside the Indonesian capital of Jakarta.

Loss of control

As a consequence, democratically elected national governments, and the people who vote for them, are no longer able to control what happens within their own boundaries. Unexpected shifts of the value of money in different countries can upset a government's economic plans. Businesses can suddenly decide to move their operations from one country to another, leaving people unemployed. The Indian government can do little about the threat that MTV poses to traditional culture. The French government is powerless to stop the French language being invaded by English words.

If decisions that affect everyone continue to be made without voters, it would seem logical to extend the voter's reach internationally, to create democratic international institutions. Some small progress in this area has been made. For example, the arrest of the former Yugoslav leader Slobodan Milosevic on charges of crimes against humanity showed that the principle of accountability—holding people responsible for their actions—could reach across international boundaries.

Former Yugoslav president Slobodan Milosevic appeared before the United Nations War Crimes Tribunal at the Hague in July of 2001.

Like the richer classes of the nineteenth century, the richer nations of the 21st century are afraid of what the majority might do if given an equal vote. As a result, there is a fear of giving international groups democratic powers as well.

International democracy?

There are no absolutely democratic international institutions representing the individual people of the world on an equal basis. The United Nations was set up in 1945 to promote international peace and cooperation. It has majority voting for nations in its General Assembly, but the effectiveness of this is severely limited by the **veto,** which five nations (the United States, Russia, Great Britain, France, and China) have in the Security Council. Also, small nations are subject to all sorts of economic pressure from the larger, richer nations.

Flies caught in a web

"What influence do politicians really have in a world of global capitalism? Single-handedly, not much .... Governments are now like flies caught in the intricate web of the market. And voters see their powerlessness. They sense that politicians' hands are tied and that their promises are increasingly empty. They watch politicians dancing to the corporations' tunes .... And so, increasingly, they are turning their backs on politics."

(Noreena Hertz in *The Silent Takeover.*)

International institutions set up to regulate international business are either not accountable, like the World Trade Organization, or only marginally democratic, like the European Union.
The European Union has a powerful appointed commission that plans and implements policies; a powerful council of ministers who are national leaders, and who decide which policies will be implemented; and a weak democratically elected parliament, which operates as a debating chamber but cannot make laws. As of right now, the chance of establishing an elected European government, able to make decisions that affect all of Europe, does not seem likely.
The chances of establishing elected global organizations that perform a similar role in the world look even worse.

When it comes to dealing with problems that cross national boundaries, only a few undemocratic international bodies, controlled by the richest states, and a large number of corporations that only have to answer to their shareholders, have any real power or influence.

The consequences of failure

This situation has obvious consequences. The first is that people have begun to realize that their elected governments have much less power and influence than before. Because of this, national politics have come to seem increasingly irrelevant to many voters, with the result that both party membership and turnout at elections have decreased at an alarming rate in many democratic countries. Some have turned to more direct forms of protest; others have simply lost interest or given up because they do not think that there is any point in getting involved in politics. Either way, democracy has been the loser.

In November of 2001, Greenpeace activists in Sydney, Australia, demonstrate against the continued hunting of whales by the Japanese.

A second consequence is that the problems created by globalization are either being handled in the interests of a few or not being handled effectively. Economic growth has created serious environmental problems, many of which need to be tackled at the international level. **Global warming,** for example, will ultimately affect most people on the planet, but the government of the Maldives, whose country may be flooded by the rising ocean levels, has no influence over those countries whose industrial pollution is causing the problem. A voluntary agreement to limit this pollution was actually reached at Kyoto in 1997, but in 2001, President Bush announced that the United States would not be approving the deal. Inside a democratic nation-state it would be impossible for such a small minority to rule over the majority in this way.

⑩ So, What is Democracy?

In 1863, the President Abraham Lincoln defined democracy as government of the people, by the people, and for the people. This might have been possible in the small city-states of ancient Greece, but in large societies, the most we can hope for is government by the chosen representatives of the people in the interests of the people. These representatives are not required to do what the people (or even a majority of the people) want them to do in any particular situation, but they are expected to carry on the business of government in general agreement with the people's wishes. If they do not, they can expect to be replaced by others who promise they will.

The recipe for democracy

In order to work, representative democracy requires a system of institutions and rules called a **constitution.** Though not always in writing, this will lay down how and when elections will be conducted, and which of many alternative voting systems will be used. Those elections will usually be contested by parties representing different sets of ideas and interests. All adults will be able to vote.

Other ingredients are also necessary. Without freedom of expression, assembly, and association, it would be impossible to have the well-informed debates that allow people to cast a meaningful vote. Without the **rule of law,** there is no guarantee that these freedoms will be upheld, that elections will be conducted fairly, or that their result will be accepted.

The system will work better in some conditions than in others. Democracy will flourish where there are no threats from the outside, where armed forces are obedient to civil (not military) government, where the

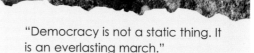

"Democracy is not a static thing. It is an everlasting march."

(President Franklin D. Roosevelt, pointing out in a speech in October of 1935 that democracy can never be taken for granted, and can always be improved.)

people have long agreed it is the only acceptable way to run things, where important political and religious values are shared, and where there is some measure of economic equality. It will struggle to survive where enemies threaten, where armed forces have influence over civil affairs, where a significant number of people still believe there is an alternative, where important values are not shared, or where there is a wide degree of economic inequality.

The **capitalist**, free **market economy** both encourages democracy by distributing decision-making and discourages it by promoting inequality. Some freedoms are also not what they seem. The freedom to support a party of your choice financially is a good example. An individual voter handing over a few dollars is contributing to the democratic process; a corporation handing over millions is trying to bribe a future government, hurting the democratic process.

A huge crowd in the Czechoslovak capital of Prague celebrates the fall of communism and the country's imminent return to democracy in November of 1989. In 1993, Czechoslovakia peacefully split into two states: the Czech Republic and Slovakia.

Are you living in a democracy?

So how can you tell if you are living in a democracy? Imagine a country with a long-established democratic constitution, well-organized political parties, an educated population, and a long history of respect for the rule of law. In this country, the media is dominated by a few companies, the major parties have very similar policies, and there is a growing gap between rich and poor. Is it a democracy?

Our imaginary country could be either the United States or Britain, both countries that like to think of themselves as democracies. Some parts of the description support that view, other parts raise doubts. It is perhaps more useful to think of democracy as a job that is far from finished, to remember how much less democratic these two countries were 100 years ago, and to imagine how much more democratic they might make themselves in the future. Many people would consider having six out of ten democratic characteristics a decent score for the beginning of the 21st century.

The prospects

Will this score rise? Some observers are optimistic. They point out how many countries have made the transition from dictatorship to democracy, particularly in the last few decades. Others are pessimistic. They stress the limited power of the democracies that now exist, and the new threat posed by the growing influence of multinational corporations that are not politically **accountable.** They fear that democracy is becoming something governments promise, but cannot deliver.

Time will tell. Perhaps the best clue is offered by the prehistoric hunters we encountered in Chapter Two as they sat around their fire, discussing when they were going to hunt the next day. They instinctively knew that using everyone's knowledge and experience would give them a better chance of eating tomorrow. Ten thousand years later, democracy still offers the best chance of fulfilling the promise of every human being.

Timeline

c. 550–10 B.C.E.	Roman Republic
c. 507–321 B.C.E.	Greek city-states adopt limited form of democracy
c. 930–1230	Icelandic Althing
1215	Magna Carta is signed at Runnymede between King John and the English barons
c. 1300	Assemblies called by Edward I grow into the English **parliament**
c. 1450	Representative assembly in Sweden
1642–49	English **civil war**
1649	Execution of King Charles I
1688	The Glorious Revolution in England and Wales
1776	U.S. Declaration of Independence from Britain
1788	U.S. **Constitution** is adopted; white male property owners can vote
1789–94	**French Revolution**
1793	New French constitution (briefly) gives the right to vote to all men
1800–30	Individual U.S. states give vote to all free white men
1832	1st Reform Act in Britain gives the vote to small landowners and some tenant farmers
1856	Australia introduces the **secret ballot**
1861–65	U.S. civil war; south not permitted to secede
1867	2nd Reform Act in Britain gives the vote to male householders in towns and more tenant farmers
1869	Fifteenth Amendment to the U.S. Constitution gives black men the right to vote; in many places, this is not enforced until 1965
1872	Britain introduces the secret ballot
1884	U.S. introduces the secret ballot
	3rd Reform Act in Britain gives the right to vote to all male householders
1893	New Zealand becomes the first country to give women the right to vote
1902	Australian women get the right to vote
1906	Finland becomes the first European country to give women the right to vote

1914–18	World War I
1917	Russian Revolution
1918	All men, and all women over 30, are given the right to vote in Britain
1920	All women in the U.S. are given the right to vote
1922	Fascism comes to power in Italy
1928	All women over 21 are given the right to vote in Britain
1933	**Nazism** comes to power in Germany
1939–45	World War II; fascism and Nazism defeated
c. 1947–87	**Cold War**
1965	The Voting Rights Act is passed to enforce the Fifteenth Amendment in the U.S.
1968	Czechoslovakia moves toward democracy and is crushed by the Soviet Union; Civil rights movement against the **tyranny** of the majority begins in Northern Ireland
1973	Chilean democracy crushed by Chilean Army
1978–79	Students and others put up posters on Democracy Wall in Beijing
1983	Military rule gives way to democracy in Argentina
1989	Pro-democracy protests in Beijing's Tiananmen Square are crushed
1989–91	Fall of **communism** in Europe
1990	Aung San Suu Kyi's National League for Democracy wins 80percent of the seats in Myanmar's national election, but victory is not recognized by the military government
1992	Algerian elections cancelled when Islamic fundamentalists seem sure to win
1994	African National Congress wins first democratic election in South Africa
2000	George W. Bush elected U.S. president with fewer votes than opponent Al Gore

Sources for Further Research

Books

Bjornlund, Lydia D. *The U.S. Constitution: Blueprint for Democracy*. Farmington Hills, Mich.: Gale Group, 1998.

Harris, Nathaniel. *Democracy*. New York: Raintree Steck-Vaughn, 2001.

Hudson, David. *The Bill of Rights: The First Ten Amendments of the Constitution*. Berkeley Heights, N.J.: Enslow Publishers, 2002.

Landau, Elaine. *Presidential Election 2000*. Danbury, Conn.: Children's Press, 2002.

Ling, Bettina. *Aung San Suu Kyi: Standing Up for Democracy in Burma*. New York: Feminist Press at The City University of New York, 1999.

Rhodes, Lisa R. *Barbara Jordan: Voice of Democracy*. Danbury, Conn.: Franklin Watts, 1998.

Shuter, Jane, ed. *Helen Williams and the French Revolution*. New York: Raintree Steck-Vaughn, 1996.

Smith, Nigel. *The Houses of Parliament*. New York: Raintree Steck-Vaughn, 1998.

Steele, Phillip. *Freedom of Speech*. Danbury, Conn.: Franklin Watts, 1997.

Websites

The U.S. Constitution:
http://www.archives.gov/exhibit_hall/charters_of_freedom/constitution/constitution.html

The Democracy Network: http://www.dnet.org/

USAID: Democracy Around the World:
http://www.usaid.gov/democracy/

International Center for Human Rights and Democracy:
http://www.ichrdd.ca/flash.html

Elections Around the World: http://www.electionworld.org/

Key Figures in the History of Democracy

Anthony, Susan B. (1820–1906). Anthony was first active in the American anti-slavery and temperance (anti-alcohol) movements, but from the 1850s was mostly concerned with winning the vote for women. In 1869, she became leader of the National American Woman Suffrage Association, and in 1904 she organized the International Woman Suffrage Alliance in Berlin.

Aung San Suu Kyi. (1945–).Suu Kyi co-founded and became leader of Myanmar's National League for Democracy (NLD) in 1988. Just before the 1990 elections, she was placed under house arrest and not allowed to run. The NLD won 80 percent of the seats but its victory was not recognized by the military government. Aung San Suu Kyi's belief in democracy and non-violence won her the Nobel Peace Prize in 1991, but ten years later Myanmar was still ruled by a military **dictatorship.**

Gorbachev, Mikhail. (1931–). Gorbachev served as General Secretary of the Soviet **Communist** Party from 1985 to 1991, and as president of the Soviet Union from 1988 to 1991. He brought an end to the **Cold War** and introduced major reforms of the Soviet political and economic system. By ending the communist monopoly of power and encouraging more open government, he created the conditions for a transition to democracy in both the Soviet Union and its former junior partners in eastern Europe.

Havel, Václav. (1936–). Havel was a Czech playwright who became a spokesman for human rights and pro-democracy groups in Czechoslovakia in the 1970s. Twice imprisoned, he founded the Civic Reform group on his second release in 1989, and was prominent in the campaign for political change that culminated later that year in Czechoslovakia's peaceful transition from communism to democracy, the so-called Velvet Revolution. He became president, first of Czechoslovakia, then of the Czech Republic, after Czechoslovakia split into the Czech Republic and Slovakia in 1993.

Jefferson, Thomas. (1743–1826). Jefferson was responsible for drafting the Declaration of Independence. During discussions on the new country's **constitution,** his arguments in favor of more democracy were very influential. He stressed the need for a clear separation of powers between the arms of government, and for a decentralized **federal** system. He became president in 1801.

King, Martin Luther, Jr. (1929–68). King led the civil rights movement in the South, beginning with the Montgomery bus boycott in 1955–56, until his assassination in Memphis in 1968. His early efforts were directed toward ending racial segregation, and after proving successful in this regard he turned his attention to African-American voting rights. His 1965 campaign resulted in a Voting Rights Bill that guaranteed African Americans both the right to vote and the freedom to do so.

Mandela, Nelson. (1918–). Mandela was active in South Africa's African National Congress (ANC) beginning in the 1940s. His campaign against **apartheid** resulted in his imprisonment in 1964. On his release in 1990, he resumed leadership of the ANC and conducted the negotiations with whites which led to majority rule. In 1994 he was elected president of South Africa.

Pankhurst, Emmeline. (1858–1928). Pankhurst led the women's suffrage movement in Britain. She founded the Women's Social and Political Union in 1903, and for the next 11 years, until the outbreak of World War I, she and her elder daughter Christabel led a huge campaign for the women's right to vote which involved the imprisonment of thousands and the destruction of property.

Socrates. (*c.* 470–399 B.C.E.). Socrates was one of the most significant of the Greek **philosophers.** He was the teacher of *Plato* (*c.* 429–347 B.C.E.), whose writings contained many of the ideas of Socrates. Plato in turn was a teacher of *Aristotle* (*c.* 384–322 B.C.E.), who became tutor to Alexander the Great and wrote a huge quantity of works on a wide range of subjects, from biology to politics to poetry.

Glossary

apartheid system of enforced racial segregation in South Africa from 1948 to 1991

cabinet group appointed by president or prime minister, composed of government department heads

capitalism economic system in which the production and distribution of goods depend on private wealth and profit-making

civil war war between different groups in one country

Cold War name given to the hostility that existed between the capitalist and communist worlds between about 1947 and the late 1980s

communism originally an extreme form of socialism, in which property is held communally (in common) rather than individually. The Russian Bolsheviks, who seized power in the second Russian Revolution of 1917, renamed themselves the Russian Communist Party. The term communism became associated with the dictatorial state and system of economic planning that was created in the Soviet Union during the 1920s and '30s.

constitution in politics, the way a country is set up to safeguard its fundamental principles

corruption immoral practices like bribery and fraud

developing world countries with underdeveloped economies

dictatorship government by an individual (called a dictator) or a small group that does not allow the people to have any say in their government

executive in government, the individual or body that has the duty of introducing and enforcing new measures and laws

federal state (or federation) country made up of several states or provinces. Some powers are exercised at the central or federal level, others at the state or provincial level.

French Revolution political upsurge in France that developed into a full-scale assault on the upper classes. It ended with the 1793–94 reign of terror in which the king and many aristocrats were executed.

global warming gradual warming of Earth's atmosphere, which is mostly caused by rising levels of carbon dioxide (also called the Greenhouse Effect). The increased burning of fossil fuels (in cars, for example) and the accelerating destruction of the planet's forests are the main source of these rising levels.

House of Lords upper house of the British parliament

judiciary those responsible for administering and upholding the legal system

legislature law-making (legislative) assembly

market economy economy in which decisions are made by buyers and sellers in a free market

monarchy government headed by a monarch (king, queen, or emperor) who usually inherits the position from his or her father or mother

Nazi abbreviation (in German) for Hitler's National Socialist Party, which ruled Germany between 1933 and 1945

parliament legislative assembly that has been at least partly elected

philosopher thinker about life

proportional representation (PR) voting system that tries to ensure that the number of votes cast for each party is accurately reflected in the number of seats each party wins

Protestantism form of Christianity that split off from the Catholic church in the sixteenth century

representative democracy system in which people elect representatives to make decisions for them

rule of law situation where the law of the country is obeyed by all, including those in government and the armed services

secret ballot system in which no one knows how any particular person votes

sovereignty power

tyranny harsh and absolute rule

undemocratic not taking the electorate's wishes into account

unitary state state in which the central government has complete authority

veto right to reject a decision or proposal made by a law-making body

Index